Original title:
Beneath Frosted Skies

Author: Johan Kirsipuu
ISBN HARDBACK: 978-9916-79-648-1
ISBN PAPERBACK: 978-9916-79-649-8
ISBN EBOOK: 978-9916-79-650-4

Echoes in the Frost

Whispers weave through icy air,
Soft secrets lost in breath of dawn.
Shadows dance in frosty glare,
Nature's hush, a quiet song.

Crystal patterns grace the ground,
Footsteps lead where thoughts can roam.
In stillness, magic can be found,
Echoes call us gently home.

Glacial Dreams Awaken

Silent sighs break the night,
Wonders melt in morning light.
Dreams unfurl like snowy wings,
Born anew as twilight sings.

Glistening mists in pale embrace,
Canvases of white and blue.
In each drape, a hidden space,
Where fantasies feel true.

Underneath the Silver Canopy

Moonlight bathes the world in sheen,
Stars like diamonds softly gleam.
Underneath this silver scene,
Hearts awaken with a dream.

Branches bowed with frosted grace,
Nature's breath a whispered tune.
In this realm, we find our place,
Swaying softly, lost in moon.

Lament of the Frozen Echo

Winds of sorrow gently cry,
Haunting notes of time long past.
In their chill, memories lie,
Whispers soft, yet meant to last.

Frozen fields hold stories dim,
Each frostbite, a tale untold.
When the light grows faint and slim,
These echoes clutch a heart of gold.

The Hushed Song of a Frozen World

Silence drapes the sleeping trees,
Winter whispers on the breeze.
A blanket white, so soft, so still,
Nature's heart begins to chill.

Shadows dance in pale moonlight,
Stars flicker in the velvet night.
Footsteps crunch on snowy ground,
In this peace, a hush profound.

Frozen streams in silver flow,
Echoes of a world aglow.
As time pauses, dreams unfold,
A tale of warmth against the cold.

In the quiet, memories gleam,
A canvas painted with a dream.
The world awaits a gentle thaw,
In this frozen breath, we draw.

Wings of Gossamer Snowflakes

Gentle flakes on whispered sighs,
Drifting softly from the skies.
Like feathered dreams, they swirl and glide,
Each a treasure, winter's pride.

A tapestry of white and light,
Transforms the world, pure and bright.
With every flake, a spark of grace,
Cascading down to embrace this space.

They dance around in frosty air,
With every gust, without a care.
Nature's angels in purest form,
Creating magic, a tranquil storm.

Each crystal holds a frozen kiss,
A fleeting moment, a whispered bliss.
In their softness, stories weave,
Of ephemeral beauty we believe.

Frost-Kissed Memories

Memories wrapped in ice and pearl,
Frozen times that softly swirl.
In the corners of the mind,
Echoes of warmth, we seek to find.

Glistening scenes of days gone by,
Laughter wrapped in a wintry sigh.
Moments cherished, crystal-clear,
Captured gently, held so dear.

Shadows linger in frosted air,
Whispers of friends still linger there.
Each breath a part of the hidden past,
In the heart, these memories last.

Frosty windows, a hazy view,
With every glance, they come to you.
A tapestry of joy and pain,
In the silence, we remember again.

The Weight of Icicles on Time

Icicles hanging, heavy with fate,
Preserving moments, we contemplate.
Each droplet poised, a tale untold,
The weight of memories, gradual and bold.

Seasons shift in their silent hold,
As time unwinds, both young and old.
Nature's clock with icy chime,
Marks the passage, the weight of time.

Fragile structures, delicate and bright,
Reflect the sun, a fleeting light.
In the cold, they glisten and gleam,
A reminder of life, a flowing dream.

In their stillness, we pause and gaze,
Lost in wonder, in winter's haze.
Carved by nature, they stand and sway,
The story of time, in ice they lay.

Secrets Underneath the Chill

Whispers hide beneath the snow,
Dreams of warmth, longing to grow.
In the silence, shadows creep,
Cradling secrets the frost will keep.

Nature's breath, a frosty sigh,
Beneath the blanket, secrets lie.
Each flake tells a story old,
In winter's grasp, the world turns cold.

Branches bow with a crystal sheen,
Frozen tales of what has been.
The stillness wraps the earth in gray,
A tapestry of night and day.

Moonlight glimmers on icy streams,
Casting light on forgotten dreams.
Where solitude and beauty blend,
In winter's heart, we find a friend.

So we wander, searching deep,
For hidden truths that nature keeps.
Underneath the chill, we find,
The warmth of love that knows no bind.

Crystalline Reveries

In the stillness, crystals glow,
Reflecting dreams in moonlit flow.
Softly falling, silence reigns,
In this world where peace remains.

Glistening whispers on the trees,
Carried gently by the breeze.
Each moment feels like a sweet embrace,
In the realm of winter's grace.

Dancing lights on fields of white,
Drawing us into the night.
In the quiet, hearts take flight,
Crystalline visions, pure delight.

A tapestry of stars above,
Filling the night with endless love.
Every flicker paints a scene,
In reveries that feel serene.

As dreams are spun in icy lace,
We tread softly, find our place.
In crystalline beauty, we reside,
Forever captives of the tide.

Frosted Lanterns in the Dark

Frosted lanterns twinkle bright,
Guiding wanderers through the night.
Each light glows with a tranquil charm,
Embracing all in tender calm.

Amid the shadows, warmth appears,
Casting away our hidden fears.
In every flicker, tales unfold,
Whispers of stories, brave and bold.

Branches lace with icicles fine,
Create a world that feels divine.
A path of light through winter's chill,
Invites us onward, still and still.

Hearts aglow, we dance and sing,
Celebrating what the dark can bring.
Frosted lanterns in the mist,
Illuminate the paths we've kissed.

So let us wander, hand in hand,
Through this enchanted winterland.
For every light is hope restored,
A beacon bright, forever adored.

Glow of the Winter Moon

Underneath the winter moon,
Softly sings a distant tune.
Glowing silver on the snow,
In the stillness, dreams will grow.

Stars are scattered, coy and bright,
In the tapestry of night.
Each shimmer whispers secrets low,
Of the tales they used to know.

Shadows stretch and softly dance,
Inviting us to take a chance.
In the glow, we find our way,
To where the heart feels free to sway.

Beneath the vast and open sky,
The moonlight weaves a lullaby.
With every step, we are embraced,
By the magic of this place.

As night unfolds its jewel tones,
We gather warmth in whispered tones.
Under the glow, our spirits soar,
In winter's heart, we seek for more.

A Canvas of Slumbering Souls

In twilight's grasp, the dreams unfold,
A tapestry of whispers, softly told.
Stars weave the tales of night's embrace,
Beneath the moon, we find our place.

The air is thick with slumber's song,
As shadows dance where we belong.
Each breath a brushstroke, light and free,
Painting worlds for you and me.

In silent corners, secrets bloom,
While echoes linger in the room.
A symphony of hopes and fears,
Crafted gently through the years.

Awake, yet lost in vibrant dreams,
Where nothing's ever as it seems.
The canvas glows with phantom light,
Guiding souls through endless night.

Here in this realm, we drift and sway,
A midnight's waltz, a soft ballet.
In slumber's arms, our spirits glide,
On a canvas, wide and wide.

The Flicker of Hearth in Frost's Domain

In winter's grasp, the world stands still,
A quiet hush, the air like chill.
The hearth's bright glow, a beacon warm,
Against the night, a sheltering charm.

Snowflakes dance in whispered flight,
While shadows play in soft, dim light.
The fire crackles, stories weave,
Of warmth and love that we believe.

Outside, the frost lays its white claims,
On every branch, it softly frames.
Yet here inside, our laughter's heard,
A melody, the heart's true word.

As embers glow, the spirits rise,
Reflecting light in each other's eyes.
The flicker brightens, hopes ignite,
In frost's domain, we find our fight.

So let the cold wind howl and wail,
For here we weave our winter tale.
With every flicker, love's embrace,
In hearth's warm heart, we find our place.

Hibernation's Silent Rhapsody

In shadows deep, the world lays still,
A blanket soft, a winter's chill.
Dreams drift slow through twilight's glow,
As nature whispers, soft and low.

Frosted branches, bare and stark,
Cradle secrets in the dark.
The world holds breath, in peace confined,
A lullaby for hearts aligned.

Beneath the snow, life ebbs and flows,
Awaiting warmth from springtime's throes.
Patience reigns in cold embrace,
As time unwinds at nature's pace.

Silent echoes fill the air,
A tranquil calm, devoid of care.
In hibernation, dreams take flight,
To stir again with morning light.

When spring arrives, with vibrant cheer,
Awakening what's hidden here.
Yet in the depth of winter's night,
Exists a symphony of light.

The Frost's Gentle Touch

The dawn breaks soft, a glistening sight,
As frost adorns the world in white.
Each blade of grass, a diamond glow,
A tender gift from winter's flow.

Whispers of cold in morning air,
Brush the earth with loving care.
Nature's art, so delicate,
A fleeting moment we won't forget.

Veils of crystal lace the trees,
Dancing lightly with the breeze.
The quiet hush of winter's song,
In this serene, where we belong.

Footprints mark the path we tread,
In chilly realms where dreams are bred.
With every step, the world awakes,
Beneath the frost, a joy that quakes.

As sun dips low, the shadows grow,
The frost remains, a gentle glow.
In twilight's hold, our hearts will yearn,
For every season's soft return.

Vows of the Winter Sky

Underneath a sky of gray,
Where stars whisper at end of day.
The promise held in frosty air,
Of love eternal, pure, and rare.

Snowflakes fall like whispered vows,
Softly settling on the prow.
Each flake tells a tale of grace,
In winter's cold, we find our place.

As twilight glows, the world transforms,
In icy realms, our hearts are warm.
The quiet night embraces us,
In winter's hush, devoid of fuss.

Together, we watch the skies,
In silence shared, love never dies.
With each glance, a promise binds,
In winter's cold, our heart entines.

Seasons change, as they must do,
Yet winter's light shines ever true.
In frosty whispers, we have found,
A love that echoes all around.

The Artistry of Frozen Raindrops

Raindrops fell, then frozen fast,
Creating art that seems to last.
Each droplet caught in time's embrace,
A crystal gem, a fleeting grace.

Beneath the storm, a world transformed,
In icy sculptures, beauty formed.
Nature's brush, with colors bright,
Turns simple rain into delight.

Every glisten, every hue,
Reflects the sky's enchanting view.
In winter's breath, they dance and play,
A fleeting moment, gone away.

With every shift of light and shade,
A canvas fine, nature's parade.
As cycles change, the raindrops flow,
We treasure this, the ebb and glow.

So let us pause, admire this scene,
Where frozen drops craft what has been.
In every icicle's embrace,
Exists the art of time and space.

Whispers of Winter's Veil

Silent sighs in the frosty air,
A blanket of white, tender and rare.
Echoes of stillness, time takes pause,
Nature's hush, it whispers, it draws.

Brittle branches, dressed in frost,
A fleeting warmth, forever lost.
Under the moon's gentle embrace,
Stars twinkle softly, they leave no trace.

Footsteps muffled on powdered ground,
In the night's hush, peace is found.
Snowflakes dance with the breath of night,
Wrapped in dreams, everything feels right.

In the shimmer of dawn's first light,
Shadows retreat, banished from sight.
A canvas painted in shades of white,
Winter's whisper, pure and bright.

Embers smolder in the lost fire's glow,
Stories linger, imparting slow.
Memories twirling like flakes in the breeze,
In winter's grasp, time finds its ease.

Silent Crystals Adrift

Dancing lightly in the chilly air,
Crystals float without a care.
Fleeting moments like whispers glide,
In twilight's embrace, they softly bide.

Each flake a story, a tale untold,
Wrapped in icy lace, wonders unfold.
Glistening secrets from heavens above,
Drifting softly, a measure of love.

As evening falls with shadows deep,
Nature sighs, the world in sleep.
Crystalline beauty, fleeting and bright,
Hold onto magic in the quiet night.

With every breath, the world becomes still,
As dreams take flight on the winter chill.
In silence, the frost paints its art,
Whispers of winter, they tug at the heart.

In the hush of dawn's soft grace,
Crystals shimmer, time finds its place.
They vanish gently with the sun's rise,
Leaving behind the night's soft sighs.

Cold Embrace of Dawn

Grey horizons whisper of the night,
Daylight breaks, chasing away fright.
Frosty breath meets the warming sun,
Another journey of day begun.

Shadows retreat from the golden glow,
Softly the world begins to grow.
Each drop of dew catches the light,
In nature's arms, everything feels right.

Birds awaken, sing sweet songs of cheer,
Echoing softly, a melody near.
In the cold embrace, life starts anew,
A canvas painted in vibrant hue.

Beneath the surface, life thrums below,
In winter's stillness, the secrets flow.
Awakening dreams from slumbering night,
The dawn captivates with its warming might.

Hope unfurls like petals in bloom,
Chasing away the lingering gloom.
In the dance of light, shadows fade,
Morning whispers, a promise made.

Chasing the Snowfall

Gentle whispers in the swirling breeze,
Snowflakes twirl like a playful tease.
Children laugh in the frosty delight,
Chasing the snow as it dances in flight.

Timid flakes on a winter's day,
Cover the ground where the children play.
With each soft touch of the chilly air,
Joy of the season, beyond compare.

Every swirl tells a tale of its own,
Carpets of white softly overgrown.
In the hush of dusk, the world is still,
Chasing the snow offers moments to thrill.

Footprints echo in the fading light,
A trail of laughter in darkening night.
Braving the cold, hearts beat as one,
Chasing the snow till the day is done.

In a world adorned in a blanket clear,
Chasing those falling flakes brings cheer.
Wrapped in warmth, the heart beats proud,
In the chase of winter, joy is unbowed.

Timeless Dance of Snow and Stars

In winter's hush, snowflakes fall,
They twirl and spin, a silent ball.
Stars above blink with delight,
As darkness yields to soft, pure white.

The moon casts shadows, long and thin,
A blanket soft, where dreams begin.
The world aglow, a tranquil trance,
Nature invites us to join the dance.

Each flake unique, a story told,
In frozen time, while hearts are bold.
Beneath the chill, warmth starts to grow,
With every step in the powdered snow.

Crisp air whispers secrets so sweet,
In this realm where seasons greet.
As time stands still, we join the show,
In the timeless dance of snow and glow.

Fleeting Whispers of Chill

The morning breaks with a gentle sigh,
As frost clings tight and shivers fly.
Each breath a cloud, a fleeting tease,
The world awash in winter's freeze.

Whispers travel on air so thin,
Through trees that sway, the chill begins.
A fleeting touch, a breath so light,
Moments captured in purest white.

Wandering winds weave tales of grace,
Fleeting echoes in this cold space.
Every laugh, a sound so clear,
Resonates, though soon to disappear.

A dance of shadows, soft and meek,
Winter's language, a quiet speak.
In every chill, there's warmth to find,
If only we embrace the unwind.

The Language of Frozen Winds

The frozen winds begin to howl,
A language spoken soft and foul.
They whiz and zip through barren trees,
Carrying whispers, hints of freeze.

Each gust a message, crisp and clear,
Inviting all to pause and hear.
In every shiver, in every sigh,
The breath of nature's lullaby.

Snowflakes dance, drawn by the breeze,
In their twirls, the heart finds ease.
They weave a tapestry of white,
Filling the world with sheer delight.

With every chill, a story grows,
In the language that winter knows.
So listen well, let silence reign,
In frozen winds, find joy in pain.

Fragmented Light on Icy Ponds

The dusk descends, and colors blend,
On icy ponds where day must end.
Fragmented light, a shimmering hue,
Reflecting moments, creation's view.

Each ripple dances, a fleeting sight,
Caught in whispers of the fading light.
Memories suspended, forever saved,
In the grasp of winter, softly paved.

With twilight's brush, the edges glow,
In hues of azure, gold, and snow.
A canvas stark, yet filled with dreams,
A silent world, bursting at the seams.

Wonders captured in nature's grasp,
A fragile beauty, we hold and clasp.
As nightlings cloak the icy embrace,
Fragmented light finds its place.

A Tapestry of Ice and Time

In winter's grasp, the world unfolds,
A tapestry of ice, spun bold.
Each flake a whisper, soft and light,
Stories woven through the night.

Frozen rivers, silent as breath,
Reflect the stillness, dance with death.
A canvas pure, in white it gleams,
Fractured echoes of silver dreams.

The moonlight kisses every spire,
A glistening touch, a secret fire.
Crystals shimmer, as shadows creep,
This cosmic wonder holds my sleep.

A moment paused, a fleeting sigh,
In the quiet, time slips by.
Each heartbeat syncs with nature's rhyme,
A dance eternal, ice and time.

Mystic Shadows of the Frost

In the depths of chilling air,
Where mystic shadows writhe and dare.
The frost invites a whispered dance,
A spectral realm, a ghostly trance.

Glistening forms, both strange and bright,
Twinkle softly in the night.
They weave through trees, past ancient stone,
Creating tales of ice alone.

A mirror world in crystal laid,
Where silence hums in shadows swayed.
The moon casts dreams on snowy ground,
In frostbitten whispers, secrets found.

Echoes linger, cold yet sweet,
In every heart, the frost's heartbeat.
Harbingers of winter's grace,
In mystic shadows, we find our place.

The Gaze of Shimmering Stars

When night descends and fades the day,
The stars emerge, in swift array.
They twinkle bright in velvet skies,
A cosmic dance, where magic lies.

Each spark a dream, a wish anew,
In silken depths, a vibrant hue.
They guide our thoughts to distant lands,
In shimmering glances, fate's own hands.

Celestial whispers serenade,
In endless realms, where hopes are laid.
The vast embrace of infinite night,
Awakens hearts to purest light.

With every gaze, a journey starts,
Tracing paths through countless hearts.
The gaze of stars, eternal dance,
In every moment, a timeless chance.

Frostbitten Memories

In icy veins, memories lie,
Frostbitten moments that never die.
The chill of time wraps them tight,
Beneath the surface, they shimmer bright.

Each breath a cloud, a whisper shared,
Of laughter lost, of hearts laid bare.
Remnants cling in every flake,
Each glistening shard, a love to wake.

Old stories dance in the twilight glow,
As winter weaves its magic slow.
The chill invokes the fading light,
Within our hearts, the spark ignites.

A fragile warmth through bitter air,
In frostbitten whispers, we find care.
For every memory softly speaks,
Of love submerged, yet never weak.

Palette of Snowbound Light

In silence, white blankets fold,
Whispers of dreams, soft and bold.
The world is a canvas, pure and bright,
Painted anew in snowbound light.

Trees wear cloaks of shimmering lace,
Crystal formations, nature's grace.
Each flake a story, yet untold,
Glistening treasures, a marvel to hold.

Sunrise spills golden rays,
Through icy branches, it plays.
A dance of shadows on the ground,
In this gallery, beauty found.

Footsteps crunch on winter's art,
Every sound a beating heart.
Echoes of laughter in the air,
Joy intertwines with cold's despair.

As night descends with stars to gleam,
The world is lost in a serene dream.
A palette of colors, soft and bright,
In the quietude of snowbound light.

Murmurs in the Chilled Air

Beneath the hush of frosty skies,
Soft whispers float, where silence lies.
A breath of winter, sharp and clear,
Murmurs of magic, drawing near.

Echoes dance among the trees,
Carried lightly by chilling breeze.
A gentle sigh, the world's intent,
Nature speaks, the heart can't relent.

Moonlit shadows flicker and sway,
Guiding the lost along their way.
With every rustle, secrets shared,
In the chilled air, all souls bared.

The stars are tales of ancient lore,
While owls hoot and the night does soar.
Nestled in the velvet of night,
Murmurs weave a tapestry bright.

In this frozen, twinkling sprawl,
Hear the night's enchanting call.
Mysteries rise like mist from care,
In the whispers of the chilled air.

Fables of Frost and Flame

Fables told in the ember's glow,
A dance of ice where the warm winds blow.
The clash of seasons, bold and bright,
Frost and flame in a fiery fight.

Winds of winter weave their spell,
While hearthside tales from memory dwell.
Stories spun with a crackling sound,
In the warmth of hearts, hope is found.

Icicles hang like frozen tears,
Echoing laughter throughout the years.
A fragile balance of dark and light,
Fables of frost holding flames tight.

With every spark, a story's flight,
Guided by shadows, weaving through night.
Between the chill and the warmth's embrace,
Life's myriad tales find their place.

In every flicker, memories dance,
A harmonious blend, a perfect chance.
Embrace the warmth as the cold exclaims,
The heart remembers the fables of flames.

Shards of Winter's Tale

In the twilight, crystals gleam,
Fragments of light, a gentle dream.
Shards of winter, bright and clear,
Each one sings, a story near.

Brittle branches stretch and quiver,
Reflecting moonlight in a shiver.
Scattered pieces of silence fall,
A symphony played at nature's call.

Footprints trace a whispered quest,
Seeking solace, warmth, and rest.
Through the drifts, the heart will sail,
Unraveling shards of winter's tale.

Snowflakes flutter, a ballet divine,
Woven paths through bristles, pine.
Embers glow in the fading light,
Warming spirits on long winter nights.

In every sparkle, magic hides,
Where hope ignites and truth abides.
Through the stillness, let dreams prevail,
Embrace the shards of winter's tale.

Crystalized Visions of Tomorrow

In the shimmer of the night,
Hope glimmers like a star,
Dreams take flight on frosty winds,
Guiding hearts from near and far.

Each breath a whisper of the dawn,
Forming patterns in the air,
Mirrored visions dance and sway,
Future's promise, bold and rare.

The night's embrace is warm yet cold,
Unlocking secrets of the mind,
In the stillness, visions call,
Words unspoken, intertwined.

Stars align in gentle grace,
Crafting tales of what could be,
Frosted dreams, a world to share,
In the heart of mystery.

Awaken now, the time is here,
To chase the glimmers in the night,
Crystalized visions of tomorrow,
Are now within our grasp, in sight.

Where the Cold Embraces

In shadows deep, the chill descends,
Winter's breath, a quiet song,
Among the pines, the silence blends,
With secrets held, where dreams belong.

The frost paints lace on every branch,
A tapestry of white and gray,
In this stillness, heartbeats dance,
As nature weaves its cold ballet.

Beneath the stars, a world transformed,
The moonlight bathes the earth in glow,
In frigid air, connections warmed,
In this embrace, we come to know.

Footprints whisper on the snow,
Stories told of love and loss,
In icy realms where spirits flow,
The heart learns well to bear its cross.

Together we shall face the cold,
With warmth that kindles from within,
In the spaces where hearts unfold,
We find our solace once again.

The Lure of a Glacial Dawn

As night departs, the sky ignites,
With hues of amber, soft and bright,
A glacial dawn begins its dance,
Awakening the world from trance.

The mountains stand in shimmering white,
Reflecting dreams that feel so right,
With every ray, the shadows flee,
Embracing warmth, the soul runs free.

Whispers of ice in the morning air,
Call to hearts that yearn to dare,
To chase the light, to bear the day,
Where all the doubts shall melt away.

In every breath, the promise sleeps,
Of stories shared, of laughter deep,
A world reborn in golden hues,
Where every heart can bloom and choose.

The allure of dawn, a brand new start,
With glacial beauty, we take part,
In the rhythms of life, we find our way,
A dance of hope that will not sway.

Hazy Dreams Under Winter's Blush

In a world of muted gray,
Hazy dreams begin to play,
Fleeting visions, soft and sweet,
Under winter's tender seat.

Veils of fog entwine the trees,
Whispers carried by the breeze,
Nostalgia lingers in the air,
Stories woven with gentle care.

Pine-scented nights, a solemn peace,
Where shadows gather, fears release,
Stars like lanterns, glowing bright,
Guiding hearts through endless night.

Frozen lakes reflect the moon,
A serenade, a haunting tune,
In each ripple, secrets hide,
Underneath, the dreams reside.

Together wrapped in winter's light,
We find our solace, pure delight,
In hazy dreams, we drift and turn,
Under winter's blush, we yearn.

Elysium of Winter's Embrace

In whispers soft, the snowflakes dance,
Wrapped in silence, they take their chance.
Each flake a story, unique and pure,
Ode to the winter, serene and sure.

Under the pale, silver moon's glow,
Nature's beauty, a magical show.
Branches wear crystals, a crown of white,
Elysium calls, in the still of night.

Frozen streams hum a gentle tune,
As stars reflect in the silver boon.
In this embrace, time stops to breathe,
All hearts find solace, all troubles leave.

Winter's hush spreads peace through the land,
A tranquil moment, so soft, so grand.
Footsteps echo on paths once trod,
In the realm of frost, we feel like gods.

Elysium whispers from high above,
In winter's arms, we find our love.
A tapestry woven with threads of white,
Eternal beauty, in the heart of night.

Fragments of a Frigid Heart

In the depths of winter's bleak embrace,
Cold shadows dance, leaving nary a trace.
Frozen whispers of dreams long gone,
Echo through valleys, where hope's withdrawn.

Icicles hang like fragile tears,
A testament to forgotten years.
Each shard of ice, a memory lost,
Love's warmth dimmed, but not the cost.

Through twilight's glow, emotions freeze,
In frigid hearts, only silence breathes.
Amidst the chill, a longing grows,
For warmth and light, the heart still knows.

Yet from the frost, a spark ignites,
Glimmers of hope beneath starlit nights.
For even cold hearts can learn to thaw,
In the quiet moments, we find our awe.

Fragments may linger but strength remains,
Resilience thrives despite the pains.
In winter's grasp, we'll find our part,
Mending together a frigid heart.

The Canvas of the Cold

A canvas lies, pure and white,
Stretched beneath the starry night.
Brush of frost paints every tree,
Capturing beauty, wild and free.

Violet shadows, the moon's soft glow,
Embracing stillness wrapped in snow.
Every footprint a story shared,
In the chill of a world unprepared.

Whispers of winds through icy air,
Draw melodies that float with care.
Nature whispers, secrets untold,
As winter's magic begins to unfold.

Eyes behold the shades of gray,
Merging with dusk to chase gray away.
The canvas breathes with life anew,
Under the blanket of sky so blue.

In this masterpiece, we find our place,
Embracing the serenity, the pure embrace.
Artistry speaks in the hush of the cold,
Stories of winter, quietly told.

Celestial Dust on Ice

In realms where night and frost collide,
Celestial dust drapes the world wide.
Crystals shimmer with starlit dreams,
Whispers of magic in icy streams.

Galaxies twinkle above the frost,
In their brilliance, we cannot be lost.
Each flake a glimpse of the cosmos bright,
Carried on wings of the winter's flight.

The heavens bow to the earth below,
As silver winds weave through the snow.
Stars find solace in snowflakes' embrace,
A dance of light in this tranquil space.

Guided by whispers of celestial grace,
Footprints vanish without a trace.
In frozen realms, we dream and sigh,
As the universe wraps us, softly nigh.

Celestial dust on ice we tread,
In awe of beauty, our hearts are fed.
A harmonious blend of earth and sky,
In this winter's wonder, we dare to fly.

Ephemerality of Wintry Whispers

Beneath the snow's soft cloak, they sigh,
Fleeting moments drift and fly.
Whispers fade in winter's breath,
Life's sweet struggle, shadows' depth.

Silent trees hold secrets near,
Branches bow, yet persevere.
Winter's hush, a tender spell,
Ephemeral tales, hard to tell.

Footsteps crunch on snowy ground,
Echoes of a world unbound.
Chill winds weave through every bough,
Time moves slowly, feel it now.

Luminous stars blink above,
Frozen night, a gentle love.
In the dark, a faint glow gleams,
Whispers weave through quiet dreams.

As dawn breaks, the mist ascends,
Winter's tale, it never ends.
Softly melts the crystal hue,
A fleeting beauty, fading too.

Elegy to the Glacial World

In icy halls of silent grace,
Nature whispers, leaves a trace.
The glacier's heart, a timeless flow,
In its tears, the past will show.

Snowflakes dance on winter's air,
Tender notes of cold despair.
Echoes of the ancient ice,
In their stillness, secrets lie.

Caverns hold a crystal light,
Fractured dreams of day and night.
Time erodes, but memories stay,
Frozen tales of yesterday.

Every shard, a history,
Whispered winds, soft elegy.
Glacial dreams, a quiet sigh,
Silent witness to the sky.

Beneath the frost, life holds tight,
Even in the darkest night.
An elegy to worlds once bold,
Now encased in frozen gold.

Reflections on a Crystal Lake

Beneath the surface, secrets gleam,
A quiet world, a tranquil dream.
Reflections dance, a mirrored sky,
Time stands still as moments fly.

Ripples whisper, soft and low,
Glimmers scatter, play and glow.
Nature's palette, pure and bright,
In this haven, hearts take flight.

Frozen breath upon the glass,
Time's embrace, a tender pass.
Echoes of the day unfold,
Stories waiting to be told.

In twilight's shade, the colors blend,
A sacred space where souls commend.
Crystal lake, a peace profound,
In your depths, love can be found.

As the stars begin to rise,
Shimmers mimic evening skies.
Reflections hold a fleeting spark,
In the night, your essence larks.

Lullabies of the Evening Chill

As twilight cloaks the fading sun,
Lullabies of dusk begun.
Evening chill wraps all in gray,
Whispered dreams lead hearts away.

Breezes coil through branches bare,
Softly singing to the air.
In the quiet, stories creep,
Cradled deep in nature's sleep.

Frosty fingers touch the ground,
Nature hums a lullaby sound.
Under stars, the world exhales,
In its rest, a magic trails.

Moonlight spills on silent snow,
Gentle glow, a soft hello.
Evening's peace, a tender thrill,
Wrapped in warmth, the night stands still.

Lullabies weave through the night,
Promising the dawn's first light.
In the hush, dreams take their flight,
Whispers linger, soft and bright.

Frosted Wishes in the Night Air

In the stillness of the night,
Whispers dance in silver light,
Frosted dreams on softest breath,
Hushed by the chill, they flirt with death.

Glistening paths of purest white,
Guide the heart through winter's bite,
Each wish carried on the breeze,
Cradled gently by the trees.

Stars shimmer like a distant flame,
Calling softly by their name,
Wrapped in warmth, though shells are cold,
Tales of hope through silence told.

Branches draped in crystal lace,
Nature's beauty, tranquil grace,
Frosted wishes take to flight,
In the magic of the night.

From the shadows emerges light,
As winter sings its heart's delight,
Each twinkle echoes through the dark,
Frosted wishes leave their mark.

The Unseen Magic of Chill

Gentle whispers in the breeze,
Creeping softly through the trees,
A touch of frost, a breath of air,
Unseen magic floating there.

Crystals form on window panes,
Nature's art that never wanes,
Silhouettes in shadows cast,
Moments fleeting, memories last.

The world asleep beneath a sheet,
Of glistening white, a winter treat,
In every flake, a story sings,
Of unseen magic that winter brings.

Sparks of chill that weave and glide,
Across the earth, a frosty tide,
In the silent, cold embrace,
Lies enchantment, full of grace.

As night descends with velvet cloak,
The air alive, a mythic smoke,
Each breath a secret waiting still,
In the unseen magic of chill.

Glimmers of Warmth in a Sea of Ice

Amid the ice, where shadows play,
Glimmers of warmth chase night away,
A fire's glow, a flickered spark,
Guides the heart through winter dark.

In every breath, a story lies,
Of warmth that echoes through the cries,
Beneath a blanket cold and white,
Hope springs forth, a gentle light.

Each frozen branch, a tale unwound,
Of hidden strength beneath the ground,
Glimmers rise from deep within,
In freezing breaths, new dreams begin.

A symphony of frost and flame,
Each moment treasured, none the same,
Dancing flames against the chill,
Soft glimmers forging passion's will.

In this sea of ice, we find,
The warmth that binds both heart and mind,
Through winter's grasp, we forge our way,
With glimmers of hope to light our sway.

The Thrall of Winter's Solstice

In the hush of winter's night,
Holds the thrall of purest light,
Count the stars, a sparkling crowd,
Underneath the silken shroud.

Solstice whispers secrets old,
In the chill, both fierce and bold,
Time stands still, the world does breathe,
Wrapped in dreams that winter weaves.

Each snowflake falls, a tender kiss,
Crafting magic, pure bliss,
In the dark, find joy in pain,
As life renews through frost and rain.

Beacons of warmth in winter's clutch,
Hearts ignite with tender touch,
In the thrall, we learn to see,
The beauty wrapped in mystery.

Gather close, let spirits rise,
In the night, beneath the skies,
Winter's song, a solemn call,
The thrall of solstice, binding all.

Lanterns of Frosted Light

In the stillness of the night,
Lanterns glow, a soft delight,
Frosty whispers in the air,
Guiding travelers with care.

Underneath the silver moon,
Shadows dance, the frost a tune,
Light reflects on icy streams,
Carving paths through glassy dreams.

Crystals hanging from the trees,
Carried softly on the breeze,
Each glimmer tells a tale so bright,
Of winter's grace, of purest light.

Footprints crunch on frozen ground,
Echoes of serenity found,
In this realm where magic plays,
Lanterns warm the coldest days.

Joy resides in frosted glow,
As hearts ignite in winter's flow,
Together we find warmth and cheer,
Under lanterns shining clear.

Heartbeats of a Frozen Universe

In the depths where silence reigns,
Frozen worlds with subtle chains,
Every heartbeat, cold yet bright,
Whispers pulse through the night.

Stars that twinkle in their sleep,
Light years far, like secrets keep,
Galaxies of icy grace,
Woven truths in vast embrace.

Crystallized in cosmic dance,
Dreams awake, we take our chance,
To explore the frozen seas,
Where heartbeats echo with the breeze.

Every breath, like snowflakes fall,
Cascading softly, nature's call,
In the universe, vast and wide,
Cold embraces, love can't hide.

So let us wander, hand in hand,
Through this poem of frozen land,
With heartbeats strong, we'll dare to roam,
In a universe, we find our home.

Shattered Ice Dreams

Fragments dance in winter's light,
Shards of dreams, both bold and bright,
In the silence, stories weave,
Of hope that never dares to leave.

Mirrored reflections softly gleam,
Echoes of a silent dream,
Breaking through the ice so clear,
Whispers of what we hold dear.

Each fracture tells a tale of old,
Moments captured, brave and bold,
In the glimmer, shadows play,
Remnants of a yesterday.

Feel the chill run through our veins,
In these shapes, the heart remains,
Within the shards, we find our light,
Shattered dreams can shine so bright.

So gather 'round the frozen glow,
In shattered beauty, let love flow,
For every piece that breaks apart,
Holds a whisper of the heart.

The Language of Chill and Light

Silent echoes fill the night,
Words unspoken, chill and light,
Frozen moments softly dare,
To whisper truths beyond compare.

In the frost, a tale unfolds,
Of shadows cast and dreams retold,
A language shared with whispered breath,
In icy silence, we conquer death.

Light dances on the frozen streams,
Illuminates our hidden dreams,
With every flicker, a spark ignites,
The language of our starry nights.

In chill's embrace, we find our peace,
A stillness where all troubles cease,
Together we speak this language bright,
Of chill and warmth, of day and night.

So hold my hand, let's walk this path,
Through winter's cold, we'll share our laugh,
For in the language of our souls,
Chill and light make us whole.

Cold Clarity in the Light of Day.

In the morning's crisp embrace,
Shadows dance with muted grace.
Frosted branches gleam so bright,
Nature's breath a fleeting sight.

Whispers float on winter's breeze,
As the world bows down to freeze.
Footsteps crunch on frozen ground,
In this stillness, peace is found.

Light breaks through the silver clouds,
Casting warmth on icy shrouds.
Each drop of dew, a crystal tear,
Reflecting dreams that disappear.

As the sun begins to rise,
Hope awakens, softly sighs.
Clarity in glistening hue,
Day unfolds, serene and true.

Winter's chill begins to fade,
In the light, new paths are laid.
With each moment, hearts ignite,
Cold turns warm in day's pure light.

Silent Whispers in the Snow

Snowflakes fall like softest dreams,
Blanketing the world in gleams.
Silent whispers, secrets shared,
In the stillness, none were spared.

Shadows dance 'neath twilight's glow,
Nights adorned in purest snow.
Pine trees wear their frosty crowns,
In quiet beauty, nature drowns.

Every flake a tale untold,
In their descent, mysteries unfold.
Footprints lead through frozen glades,
Where silence breathes and time cascades.

Stars twinkle in the velvet night,
A tranquil world, serene and right.
Whispers carried on the breeze,
As the heart finds gentle ease.

Wrapped in this enchanting space,
Every moment a soft embrace.
Silent whispers linger low,
In the magic of the snow.

Echoes of Winter's Lament

Through the trees, a hollow sound,
Echoes bounce from ground to ground.
Winter's song, both sharp and clear,
In its chill, I sense my fear.

Frosted winds begin to wail,
Carrying a ghostly tale.
Leaves once bright now lie in heaps,
As the solemn silence weeps.

The sun dips low, a fading star,
Leaving shadows near and far.
In the dusk, the cold sets in,
Lingering where warmth has been.

Every echo tells a story,
Of the past and lost glory.
Footsteps fade in drifting snow,
Leaving whispers, soft and low.

Yet among the winter's sigh,
Seeds of hope begin to lie.
In the silence, dreams lament,
Yet each ending hints content.

Dreams Wrapped in Ice

In the stillness of the night,
Dreams encased in frosty light.
Shimmers dance on frozen streams,
Where reality meets its dreams.

Every breath, a plume of white,
Caught in moments, pure delight.
Veils of silence, soft and thin,
Wrap the space where thoughts begin.

Icicles hang like silver threads,
Crafted stories, gently spread.
In this realm of crystal clear,
Visions linger, close yet near.

Winds whisper secrets long since told,
Carried on the chill, so bold.
Each dream wrapped in winter's grace,
Offers warmth in this cold place.

With the dawn, the sun will break,
Melting all that ice did make.
Yet the dreams will hold their place,
In the heart's enduring space.

Footprints Lost in Winter's Breath

In the hush of snow's embrace,
Footprints fade without a trace,
Whispers dance on icy air,
Memories linger everywhere.

Trees stand tall, their branches bare,
Crystals sparkle, cold and rare,
Silhouettes in winter's white,
Cover earth in soft delight.

A quiet world, so vast and deep,
Nature's blanket, secrets keep,
Each step echoes in the night,
A fleeting warmth, a distant light.

Restless winds weave tales anew,
Stories told in every view,
Footprints lost, we wander still,
Chasing dreams on winter's chill.

In this realm of frost and glow,
Life is paused, yet yearns to grow,
With each breath, a quiet prayer,
For spring's return, to linger there.

A Tapestry of Frozen Moments

Snowflakes fall like whispered dreams,
Stitched together in moonbeams,
Each flake tells a tale unique,
In winter's breath, we softly speak.

Frozen lakes reflect the skies,
Where silence sings and beauty lies,
Frosted fields like canvas wide,
Nature's art, a graceful guide.

Moments caught in chilly air,
Memories woven with a care,
Time stands still in this embrace,
A tapestry of serene grace.

Each footfall crunches, crisp and clear,
Echoing in the stillness near,
A season wrapped in purest white,
Holding dreams till warmth ignites.

As twilight falls, shadows bend,
The tapestry will soon transcend,
Into spring where colors bloom,
But winter's heart will hold the room.

The Still Pulse of Winter's Heart

Beneath the icy, tranquil views,
A heartbeat whispers, soft as dew,
The still pulse of a world at rest,
In chilly arms, we feel refreshed.

Crisp air fills the quiet night,
Flickering stars with gentle light,
The moonbath's glow, a silver thread,
In winter's dreams, our hopes are fed.

Branches creak with age-old tales,
Nature's sigh within the gales,
Frosty breath on winter's face,
Harmonies in cold embrace.

A silver world, both soft and stark,
Our souls ignite with winter's spark,
In stillness found, the heart can soar,
Embracing all, forevermore.

The pulse endures, a steady beat,
In winter's grace, we find our feet,
With every chill, a warmth we share,
In this still world, love lingers there.

Reflections of Stillness

In the mirror of the frozen lake,
Shimmers dance with every quake,
Reflections weave a tranquil spell,
In winter's hold, all is well.

Silent woods dressed in white,
A canvas pure, a soft twilight,
Muffled sounds, the world at ease,
Nature's breath among the trees.

Softly glows the fading sun,
Illuminating all that's done,
Each moment captured, held so dear,
In stillness found, we persevere.

A heartbeats' echo in the night,
Reflections guide with gentle light,
In the calm, we find our way,
Winter's charm, a dance of gray.

Seasons turn, yet memories gleam,
In the depths of every dream,
Stillness whispers, ever near,
In winter's glow, our thoughts are clear.

Shimmering Veils of Morning Mist

Gentle whispers brush the trees,
Veils of fog dance on the breeze.
Sunlight glimmers, soft and shy,
Waking dreams in the morning sky.

Meadows dressed in silver hue,
Awakening the world anew.
Birds are singing, clear and bright,
Heralding the day's first light.

The river sparkles, flows so free,
Reflecting nature's majesty.
Every leaf a diamond bright,
Catching drops of dawn's soft light.

As shadows fade, the world unfolds,
Echoes of stories yet untold.
In the stillness, peace we find,
In shimmering veils, hearts intertwine.

With every step, a world is born,
In morning's mist, we are reborn.
In nature's arms, our souls take flight,
Wrapped in dreams of pure delight.

Secrets Cradled in the Chill

In the silence of the cold,
Whispers of the night unfold.
Secrets hidden, soft and deep,
In the stillness, shadows creep.

Frosted branches, fragile grace,
Time unfolds at a slower pace.
Moonlight drapes a silver gown,
Hiding tales of joy and frown.

Each breath crystallizes in the air,
Painting frost with gentle care.
Nature's canvas, stark and bright,
Holding secrets of the night.

A lone owl calls, the echo spreads,
In the chill where silence treads.
Under starlit skies we roam,
Finding solace, feeling home.

Beneath the chill, warmth still grows,
In quiet hearts, the love still flows.
Together here, we will remain,
Cradled in the night's refrain.

Frostbitten Paths of Solitude

Through the woods, a lonely way,
Frostbitten paths where shadows play.
Echoes linger, soft and low,
In the silence, whispers flow.

Snowflakes drift on weary trees,
An ancient dance in the breeze.
Step by step, the heart beats strong,
In solitude, we find our song.

Crystals sparkle on frozen streams,
Reality woven into dreams.
Nature's heart, a steadfast guide,
In frostbitten paths, we confide.

Here we wander, lost in thought,
Lessons learned, battles fought.
Every footfall, deep and true,
In solitude, we start anew.

With every breath, the world feels wide,
In quiet corners, love abides.
Frostbitten paths lead us home,
Where the heart is free to roam.

The Dance of Icicles and Shadows

Icicles hang, sharp and clear,
Dancing shadows draw us near.
In the twilight's gentle glow,
Nature's art begins to show.

Winter's breath gives life to night,
Casting dreams in silver light.
With every flicker, stories share,
In the chill, we find our flare.

Broken branches, hushed and still,
Echoing the winter's chill.
The dance of shadows flits and sways,
Guided by the moon's soft rays.

Every glimmer tells a tale,
In stillness, hearts begin to sail.
In the music of the frost,
Finding beauty, never lost.

Together here, beneath the sky,
Icicles smile as shadows sigh.
In the dance, our spirits soar,
In winter's embrace, we long for more.

Twilight's Breath on a Frozen Lake

The sky drapes low, a velvet hue,
Whispers of dusk, a moment true.
Footsteps soft on icy ground,
Nature sighs, her voice profound.

Shadows stretch, the world at peace,
Time stands still, a sweet release.
Frosted breath in evening's glow,
Under stars, the silence flows.

Crimson clouds kiss the horizon,
As twilight paints each soft decision.
The lake mirrors the fading light,
A canvas born from day to night.

Beneath the ice, secrets sleep,
Ancient echoes, promises keep.
The breath of twilight, soft and clear,
Cradles dreams that wander near.

In this stillness, hope ignites,
Beneath the veil of winter's nights.
With every star that twinkles bright,
The frozen lake reflects the light.

The Stillness of Snowfall's Embrace

Gentle flakes drift from above,
A whispered gift of winter's love.
Blanketing the world in white,
A silent song wrapped snugly tight.

Each flake a story, softly spun,
Dancing down, they join as one.
Hushed are the sounds of day to night,
In their embrace, all feels right.

Trees stand tall in snowy coats,
Holding winter's tender notes.
The earth in slumber, dreams entwined,
The stillness of snow calms the mind.

Footprints vanish, lost in time,
Moments caught, a quiet rhyme.
In this peace, the heart finds grace,
Wrapped in the snow's warm embrace.

As night arrives, the moonlight glows,
Casting shadows, as beauty shows.
In winter's arms, we softly sway,
In the stillness, we find our way.

Lullabies of a Winter's Night

When moonlight bathes the sleeping trees,
Winter sings on a gentle breeze.
A lullaby of stars so bright,
Cradles dreams through the winter night.

Softly falls the blanket white,
Whispers hush, the world in sight.
Snowflakes twirl in a silent dance,
In the stillness, hearts find chance.

Fires crackle with warm embrace,
While shadows flicker in the space.
Stories weave through the glowing flame,
Lullabies call each soul by name.

Outside, the cold does softly creep,
In cozy nooks, we drift to sleep.
Wrapped in warmth, the night unfolds,
In whispered dreams, sweet tales are told.

Stars above in the velvet sky,
Guide the night as owls softly fly.
With every note, the world takes flight,
In the lullabies of a winter's night.

Crystalline Echoes of Distant Stars

In the vastness, whispers gleam,
Crystalline echoes, sparking dream.
Stars like diamonds lace the dark,
Guiding hearts on a cosmic arc.

Each twinkle tells a tale so old,
Of worlds unseen and wonders bold.
With every flicker, secrets gleam,
In the silence, we chase the dream.

Galaxies swirl in graceful flight,
Bearing witness to the night.
In this expanse, our hopes align,
Cradled gently where starlight shines.

Time is lost in the depths of space,
As stardust weaves a soft embrace.
A cosmic dance, the pulse of fate,
Whispers linger while shadows wait.

From earth below, we reach so far,
Stretching hands to touch a star.
In the silence, our spirits soar,
Crystalline echoes forevermore.

Whispers in a White Wonderland

Snowflakes dance on whispers light,
In a hush of pure delight.
Trees adorned in coats of white,
Breathe in the calm of winter's night.

Footprints trace a path so clear,
Echoes of joy, laughter near.
Children play, their spirits bright,
In this wonderland of white.

With every flake, a tale is spun,
Nature's magic, a race begun.
Crisp air wraps like a warm embrace,
Heartfelt dreams in this sacred space.

Frosty breath mingles with the stars,
Below the moon, no space for scars.
In this realm, our wishes soar,
In a white wonder, we crave for more.

As dawn breaks, the world ignites,
Hope shines through, the heart invites.
In the stillness, soft and sweet,
Whispers linger, memories greet.

Shadows Play in Crystal Light

Underneath the moon's embrace,
Shadows flit in a timeless race.
Glistening paths, where dreams reside,
In twilight's glow, they turn and glide.

Branches sway in whispered tones,
Echoing soft, mysterious moans.
Each shadow dances, moves in flight,
Caught in the spell of crystal light.

Past and present intertwine,
In the silence, shadows shine.
Softly weaving through the night,
Whispers of love, wrapping tight.

Specters of the night unfurl,
In their grasp, time starts to swirl.
Hints of laughter, signs of tears,
All captured in these fleeting years.

The night sky dons its velvet cloak,
As dreams and shadows softly spoke.
In this realm of soft twilight,
Shadows play, and hearts take flight.

The Frozen Canvas of Dreams

Brushstrokes of frost on winter's breath,
Creating art in silence, depth.
A canvas white, untouched, pristine,
In this moment, magic is seen.

The world transforms under ice's wing,
Each crystal spark, a song to sing.
Nature pauses, paints our schemes,
Life unfolds in frozen dreams.

Footprints trail in a patterned maze,
Marking time in a fleeting gaze.
A masterpiece of silence, calm,
In this stillness, the heart finds balm.

Whispers of winter's gentle hand,
Awakening hopes across the land.
The frozen canvas gleams and glows,
In its embrace, imagination grows.

As the sun dips low, shadows grow,
The palette shifts; horizons glow.
In each hue, a story streams,
Brushed upon this canvas of dreams.

Echoes of Laughter in Winter's Grip

Through frosty air, echoes reside,
Laughter dances, warmth inside.
In winter's grip, we find our cheer,
Moments cherished, memories dear.

Snowflakes land, soft as a sigh,
On cheeks bright with joy, we fly.
Gathered close beside the fire,
Fueling dreams of love and desire.

Stories spun with whispers low,
As shadows flicker, embers glow.
In every chuckle, warmth we sip,
Echoes linger in winter's grip.

Time stands still in this festive place,
Hearts united, no need to race.
With every smile, the world aligns,
In laughter's echo, magic shines.

As the night deepens, spirits soar,
With each sip, we crave for more.
Together we bask in love's sweet drip,
Echoing laughter in winter's grip.

A Symphony of Ice and Light

Crystal shards shimmer bright,
Melodies of winter night.
Winds whisper through the trees,
Nature's song; a gentle freeze.

Stars twinkle in the deep,
Cold secrets, the earth keeps.
Moonlight dances on the snow,
Illuminating all below.

Icicles form like tears,
Marking the passing years.
In this symphony of chill,
Peaceful hearts find their will.

Each flake a note, pure and white,
Crafting dreams in the night.
In the stillness, harmony flows,
A world wrapped in winter's glow.

Listen close, the ice will sing,
Of hope that each spring will bring.
Through the silence, life ignites,
In a symphony of ice and light.

Heartbeats Under a Blanket of Frost

Underneath a layer white,
Hearts beat softly, outta sight.
Each pulse is a tender sigh,
Wrapped in warmth as shadows lie.

Frosty whispers fill the air,
A quiet love, a bond so rare.
Winter's breath, both crisp and clear,
Moments shared, those we hold dear.

Beneath the frost, life stirs slow,
Dreams of spring begin to grow.
Roots entwined in silent dance,
Nature's way, a second chance.

With each heartbeat, time expands,
A promise made, through time it stands.
Underneath the frosty sheet,
Love endures, unbroken, sweet.

Wrapped in nature's cold embrace,
In the heart, a sacred place.
Under frost, our spirits glow,
Together, we quietly flow.

The Quiet Resilience of Life

In the shadows, green things lie,
Waiting for the sun to rise.
In the cold, they stretch and bend,
Quiet strength that will not end.

Icicles hang like stilled breath,
Life clings tight, defying death.
Roots dig deep in frozen ground,
Resilient whispers all around.

Gentle buds push through the ice,
Promising a world so nice.
They remind us of our fight,
The quiet resilience of light.

When darkness falls and storms arrive,
In the struggle, we survive.
Like ferns that curl in winter's grasp,
We hold tight, and we clasp.

Through the frost, the spirit thrives,
A heartbeat that always strives.
Even when the cold is rife,
There's beauty in this precious life.

Enchanted Paths of Frostbitten Ferns

Through the woods, a trail unfolds,
Fern fronds glisten, secrets told.
Frost dusts each delicate leaf,
In their beauty, we find relief.

Whispers of the ancient trees,
Carried softly on the breeze.
Hidden paths, where spirits dance,
Inviting us into a trance.

Each step leaves a fleeting mark,
Echoed in the winter's dark.
Frostbitten ferns hold their ground,
Guardians of the quiet sound.

In this enchanted realm of frost,
We find the warmth that we thought lost.
Nature beckons, come and see,
Magic thrives in tranquility.

Frozen beauty calls us near,
Transforming silence into cheer.
On these paths, our hearts will yearn,
For the wisdom we'll discern.

Solstice Serenades in Silver Hues

In twilight's embrace, shadows weave,
The stars awaken, whispers believe.
Moonlight cascades on frosted ground,
Serenades echo, a soft, sweet sound.

Trees draped in silver, timeless and grand,
Nature's orchestra plays on command.
Joyful notes blend with the chill,
Embracing the night, hearts ever still.

With every breath, the season sings,
Fleeting moments, the magic brings.
In this dance of shadows and light,
We find our solace in the night.

Snowflakes twirl, a ballet divine,
Each one unique, a precious sign.
As the solstice wraps us in its glow,
We celebrate love in winter's show.

Silent wishes on a winter's breeze,
Carried softly among leafless trees.
In this hour, our dreams align,
Serenading peace, eternally fine.

Echoing Silence of a Snowy Realm

Blankets of white on the earth lie still,
Whispers of winter, time to fulfill.
In the hush of the snow, secrets abound,
Echoing silence, a soft, sweet sound.

Footsteps muffled, in wonder we roam,
Lost in the beauty, so far from home.
Each flake a promise, each drift a dream,
In this frozen world where soft glows gleam.

Frosted branches, like crystals aglow,
Nature adorned in a serene show.
The air crisp and clear, a chill in our breath,
Life pauses gently, embracing its breadth.

Fireside warmth calls us back to the light,
Wrapped in blankets, a cozy sight.
We cherish the moments, the stories we share,
In the echoing silence, we find what we care.

With each day's end, the stars start to glow,
Guided by moonlight, our hearts gently flow.
In the snowy realm where time loses track,
We find our peace, never looking back.

Hidden Dreams in Winter's Depth

Beneath the snow, where whispers lie,
Hidden dreams linger, beneath the sky.
Each blanketed layer, a story untold,
In winter's embrace, the magic unfolds.

Muffled the sounds of the world outside,
In stillness we find where secrets abide.
Sparkling glimmers on branches and leaves,
Remind us of hope that winter achieves.

Once lively gardens now rest in repose,
Nurtured by frost, where calmness bestows.
Under the surface, the pulse of the earth,
Sows hidden dreams, awaiting rebirth.

The chill in the air, a gentle caress,
Leads us to places that winter entrusts.
In quiet reflection, we wander and roam,
Finding our way to a place we call home.

Season of stillness, of waiting, of change,
A tapestry woven, unfamiliar, strange.
But in every heartbeat, the promise we'll keep,
Hidden dreams awaken from winter's deep.

Views from a Frosted Window

Through frosted panes, the world is transformed,
A canvas of wonder, beautifully adorned.
Each gentle swirl, a delicate lace,
Painting our view with a soft, warm embrace.

Outside, the whispers of winter's delight,
As snowflakes fall softly, embracing the night.
Children's laughter, a melody clear,
Echoing memories that draw us near.

Candles flicker with a warm, golden glow,
Casting soft shadows on the shimmering show.
Inside we gather, wrapped in our dreams,
As the world outside glimmers and gleams.

With each passing hour, the dusk turns to night,
Our hearts find comfort in the soft, glowing light.
Through glass we behold winter's gentle embrace,
Finding our joy in this serene, sacred space.

Snowy landscapes unfold with soft grace,
Framing the beauty of time and of place.
Through frosted windows, our spirits take flight,
In the magic of winter, our hearts feel so bright.

Enigma of the Frozen Tundra

Beneath the skies so wide and pale,
Whispers of the wind set sail.
Secrets lie in snow's embrace,
Silent realms of time and space.

Frozen spirits dance at dusk,
In the air, a fragrant musk.
Shadows stretch on icy ground,
In this beauty, peace is found.

Mountains loom like ancient dreams,
Carved by glacial silver streams.
Traces left of footprints past,
Echoes of a world amassed.

Stars ignite the velvet night,
Shimmering with a hidden light.
Beneath the frost, a pulse persists,
In nature's clutch, the heart insists.

Awakening from winter's sleep,
Ancient promises we keep.
In each flake, a story spun,
In the tundra, we're all one.

Currents of the Frigid Night

Winds howl softly through the trees,
Whispers riding on the freeze.
Moonlight dances on the snow,
Painting paths where shadows flow.

Stars like diamonds, cold and bright,
Guide the wanderers of night.
In the stillness, hearts are bold,
Voices lost in tales untold.

Ice collects on branches bare,
Nature's breath hangs in the air.
Frigid currents, soft yet strong,
Carry echoes of a song.

Silent mountains, proud and grand,
Guard the secrets of the land.
In the dark, the world reveals,
Life entwined with frost that heals.

Each step whispered through the chill,
Crystals glisten, dreams fulfill.
In the quiet, truths ignite,
Bound together, heart and light.

A Breath in the Stillness

In the hush of winter's breath,
Life pauses, defying death.
Snowflakes twirl, a soft ballet,
Crystalline in their display.

Echoes dance upon the breeze,
Frozen moments, time's sweet tease.
In the twilight's gentle hold,
Whispers of the night unfold.

Footsteps crunch on hefty drifts,
Nature's gifts in silent shifts.
Stars above begin to gleam,
Lighting every frozen dream.

Moonlit shadows softly creep,
In this magic, secrets keep.
Each breath a story unconfined,
A tapestry of night entwined.

Here in stillness, truths align,
Frozen echoes, pure and fine.
Wrap me in your soft embrace,
In this stillness, find my place.

The Frosted Canvas of Night

A canvas stretched beneath the stars,
Frosted whispers, silver scars.
Painted in a chill so deep,
Nighttime secrets softly creep.

Brush of wind through branches weeps,
Nature's art in silence sleeps.
Colors blend in shades of blue,
A tapestry of ghosts in dew.

Icy tendrils cradle dreams,
Moonlight glistens on the streams.
In this beauty, hearts ignite,
Lost in wonder, pure delight.

Shimmering trails of sparkles roam,
Each flake a whisper calling home.
In the air, a promise glows,
Through the night, the magic flows.

The world transforms in frosty hues,
Embracing all with tender views.
In the silence, we unite,
On this frosted canvas bright.

The Crystal Quietude

In the heart of the still night,
Whispers dance on gentle breeze.
Stars twinkle with soft delight,
Dreams drift like leaves on trees.

Moonlight weaves a silken thread,
Painting shadows on the ground.
In this calm, the world feels spread,
Where silence sings without a sound.

Frosted edges kiss the dawn,
As the world begins to wake.
In this peace, all cares are gone,
Every moment, ours to take.

Nature hums a timeless song,
Echoes of a world so old.
In this realm, where we belong,
Every heart will find its gold.

Let us linger in this trance,
Where the crystal stillness glows.
In this place, we take our chance,
To embrace what nature shows.

Shadows in the Nipping Air

Whispers trail as twilight falls,
Chill winds carry secrets tight.
Underneath the ancient walls,
Shadows play with fading light.

Frosty breaths weave patterns round,
As the world dons winter's shawl.
Echoes of a past resound,
In the quiet, softly call.

Hushed steps on the frozen ground,
Footprints lost in time's embrace.
Every shadow spins around,
In this dance, we find our place.

Nipping air bites at our cheeks,
Yet, warmth stirs within our soul.
In the silence, freedom speaks,
Leading us towards our goal.

Hold my hand through dusky dreams,
Where the night and hope entwine.
In the dark, a light still gleams,
Guiding us through every sign.

A Realm of Faint Hues

Brushstrokes of a soft sunset,
Colors blend in tranquil streams.
A palette perfect, no regret,
Here we wander through our dreams.

Lavender skies and rose-tipped clouds,
Echoes of the day's soft sigh.
In this world, we stand so proud,
Where the hues of hope can fly.

Past the hills of emerald green,
Whispers beckon, secrets shared.
In the twilight, life serene,
Every moment, love declared.

In a realm of faint embraces,
Time drips slowly, sweet and pure.
Finding truth in gentle traces,
We uncurl, our hearts assured.

Brighten shadows with your laughter,
Let it ripple through the air.
In this canvas, hereafter,
We paint life beyond compare.

Horizons Anchored by Frost

When night drapes its silver veil,
Stars are fastened by the cold.
Horizons whisper quiet tales,
Of a world both young and old.

Underneath the glowing sky,
Frosty breath gives life anew.
Dreams arise and softly fly,
Just to dance where shadows grew.

Chill and warmth collide with ease,
In the stillness, hearts ignite.
Nature's canvas, painted freeze,
Calls us forth into the light.

Here, the landscape feels alive,
Every breath a story told.
In this realm, our souls revive,
Anchored by the frost's firm hold.

Let us wander hand in hand,
Through each moment, fiercely caught.
In the beauty of this land,
Find the warmth we always sought.

Icy Echoes of Forgotten Realms

Whispers dance in frosted air,
Memories haunt the silent night.
Shadows play with frozen light,
Lost within a chilling stare.

Time stands still in this vast space,
Echoes of a world long gone.
In the stillness, dreams have drawn,
Faded traces, a ghostly trace.

The moon's gaze reveals the past,
In the ice, secrets reside.
Lurking where the spirits bide,
Haunted stories, unsurpassed.

Echoes call from icy mists,
Step by step, I venture near.
A shiver dances, chills the fear,
In the silence, fate twists and twists.

Through the cold, I wander forth,
In pursuit of what was lost.
Each breath lingers, counting cost,
Yearning for the warmth of worth.

The Caress of Winter Winds

Gentle breaths of winter sigh,
Softly kissing every tree.
Murmurs in a symphony,
Nature whispers, passing by.

In the twilight's silver glow,
Frostbites dance on lips of air.
Chill of night and gentle care,
Touch of grace in falling snow.

Windswept dreams on barren lands,
Echoes of a warmth once known.
Shivers trace on skin alone,
Softly held by unseen hands.

Blades of grass wear crystal crowns,
Each blade sways to nature's song.
In the stillness, all belong,
Winter's beauty knows no bounds.

With each gust, the world will change,
Embracing all in cold delight.
Every breath, a wish ignites,
In the dance of white and range.

Celestial Dreams in Susurrus

Stars align in gentle hush,
Dreams take flight on midnight's breeze.
Secrets whispered through the trees,
A cosmic dance within the rush.

Galaxies in shades of gray,
Twinkling soft, a distant song.
In their light, we all belong,
Guided by the night's ballet.

Floating on a starlit sea,
Waves of wonder brush the soul.
In this gaze, we find our goal,
To chase the dreams that set us free.

Soft exchange in twilight's glow,
Each heartbeat a cosmic ring.
Listen close to what they sing,
In this realm, desires flow.

Celestial whispers intertwine,
Carried forth on breezes mild.
In the night's embrace, we're wild,
Chasing dreams through silver shine.

Ballet of Glacial Visions

Icebound art in silent grace,
Figures twirl in frozen air.
Nature's dance, a twinkling flare,
Ballet etched upon this space.

With each step, a crystal spark,
Ethereal movements seen.
In the glow, a world pristine,
Beauty drapes the cold and dark.

Frozen echoes softly call,
Whispers in the frosty night.
A spectacle of sheer delight,
Leaving footprints, ephemeral.

Glimmers weave through icy seams,
A language wrapped in frost and light.
Weaving tales in purest white,
A dance that shimmers, yet redeems.

In this realm, where moments freeze,
All the world a stage of mist.
Time will swirl and then assist,
In the ballet of the trees.

The Veil of White Enchantment

A blanket soft, the world subdued,
With whispers light, and magic brewed.
In frosted dreams, the silence speaks,
Each flake a tale, the heart then seeks.

In crystal nights, the stars ignite,
A dance of shadows, pure and bright.
Lost in the glow, the spirits roam,
In winter's grasp, we find our home.

The trees wear coats of shimmering white,
They beckon softly in the night.
With every breath, the air turns rare,
In this enchanted, frozen air.

Footprints trail in the morning dew,
A fleeting glimpse of joy anew.
With every twinkle, dreams expand,
As life unfolds, like magic planned.

So let us dance, in twirling grace,
Embrace the chill, this wondrous space.
For in the veil, we find our bliss,
In every sigh, a winter's kiss.

Winter's Quiet Soliloquy

The snowflakes fall, a soft refrain,
Each whispering truth, a sweet disdain.
In solitude, the world stands still,
Listening close, to nature's will.

The brook lies frozen, a silent song,
A memory held, where it belongs.
The branches sway, in muted grace,
As shadows dance across the space.

A candle flickers, a warm embrace,
In shadows cast, I find my place.
With every flick, a thought unwinds,
In winter's hold, my spirit finds.

The stars above in cobalt skies,
Reflect the dreams the heart denies.
With every glance, a wish is made,
In quiet moments, secrets fade.

So speak to me, oh winter night,
Your gentle hush, my heart's delight.
In your stillness, I find the spark,
A fragile hope, in the quiet dark.

Beneath the Silvered Canopy

Amidst the trees, a wonder grows,
In silver light, the stillness flows.
Beneath the boughs, where shadows play,
A hidden path leads dreams away.

The moonlight weaves through leaves of frost,
In whispered tales, the night embossed.
Each rustling branch, a story told,
Of time and space, in silence bold.

At twilight's edge, the magic sings,
As nature shares her gentle wings.
With every breath, I taste the night,
In silvered dreams, the heart takes flight.

The world lies hushed, in silver sheen,
Each moment carved, as if to glean.
With love and hope, we wander near,
In this embrace, I hold you dear.

So let us wander, hand in hand,
Beneath the trees, in dreamland stand.
For in the quiet, we shall find,
The silvered spell that binds our minds.

Hearts Adrift in Icy Silence

In winter's chill, our hearts do meet,
Adrift like clouds, we float on heat.
With every beat, the silence swells,
A love that breathes and softly dwells.

The frost adorns each window pane,
Reflecting dreams, like whispered rain.
In icy stillness, secrets brew,
A bond unbroken, pure and true.

Beneath the stars, in quiet gaze,
We find our warmth in winter's maze.
With every glance, the world dissolves,
A tapestry that love resolves.

In tangled limbs, we weave our way,
Through frosty nights and brightening day.
With every sigh, the cold retreats,
In this embrace, the heart repeats.

So let the winter call our name,
In love's embrace, we play the game.
For hearts adrift, will never part,
In icy silence, we find our heart.

Footprints in the Icy Silence

Silent steps crunching cold ground,
Whispers of footsteps, barely found.
Beneath the moon's watchful gaze,
Shadows dance in the frosty haze.

Frozen breath hangs in the night,
Every sound a delicate fright.
Footprints mark where I have been,
Lost in thought, the world feels thin.

The icy stillness wraps me tight,
Encasing dreams in silver light.
Echoes linger, then drift away,
In the chill, my heart wants to stay.

Fields adorned in diamond dust,
Nature's glory, pure and just.
Each imprint tells a tale anew,
Of the journey, of the view.

The night's embrace, gentle and bold,
Keeps secrets that the dawn will hold.
With every step, a life unfolds,
In icy silence, beauty molds.

The Dreamscape of Snowflakes

In the hush, soft flakes descend,
Whirling gently, they twist and bend.
A symphony of white in flight,
Crafting dreams through day and night.

Each flake a whisper, unique in form,
Spiraling down, a graceful swarm.
They dance on air, a fleeting chance,
Inviting hearts to join the dance.

Blankets of beauty, soft and wide,
Hiding the world, our hearts collide.
In the stillness, we pause and stare,
Transfixed by the magic in the air.

Winter's canvas, pure and bright,
Stories woven in pale white light.
Dreams alight on each little crest,
In this silence, we find our rest.

With every flake that drifts like time,
We lose ourselves in a world sublime.
Painting pictures in our mind's eye,
In the dreamscape where we fly.

Waiting for Thaw

Crisp air whispers of coming change,
Sunlight beckons, sweet and strange.
Branches bow beneath the weight,
The end of winter, we await.

Time drips slowly, days stretch long,
Nature stirs, begins to throng.
Underneath the frozen crust,
Hope awakens, rise we must.

Green shoots peek through white and gray,
As if to chase the cold away.
Each warm breeze turns dreams to flow,
In the soil, life starts to grow.

Ponds are whispering of release,
As daylight swells, bringing peace.
Waiting for thaw, we hold on tight,
To the promise of warmer light.

With every sunrise, warmth enthralls,
Melting echoes of winter's calls.
We gather strength, both near and far,
In the thawing, life's reset star.

The Allure of White Horizons

Endless stretches of gleaming white,
Call to wander, pure delight.
Horizon blurs with the sky above,
Inviting hearts to seek and love.

Each step forward, a hushed embrace,
In the vastness of time and space.
Snow-covered dreams that shimmer bright,
Whisper secrets from day to night.

Mountains stand like guardians tall,
Silent witnesses to it all.
Nature's wonder, vast and grand,
Hold my breath, revere this land.

The allure calls with every sigh,
Where dreams and reality lie.
A canvas wide, endless and true,
In the white horizons, I renew.

With every glance, my spirit soars,
Across the vast, uncharted shores.
In this beauty, I find my way,
The allure of snow, my heart's ballet.

Harmony in the Stillness

In quiet woods, the soft winds sigh,
As trees stand tall, beneath the sky.
Birds whisper secrets, soft and sweet,
Nature's chorus, a tranquil beat.

A brook flows gently, a silver thread,
Cradled by earth, where dreams are bred.
Every leaf hums a lullaby,
In this stillness, spirits fly.

Stars peek softly, twinkling bright,
Casting shadows in the moonlight.
Whispers linger, tender and clear,
In harmony, the world draws near.

Time pauses here, moments unfold,
Stories told in silence bold.
A tapestry woven with grace and care,
In stillness, love dances in the air.

United in peace, we find our place,
Wrapped in the warmth of a soft embrace.
The heart's desire, deep and true,
In harmony, we start anew.

The Unseen Dance of Winter

Snowflakes twirl in the moonlit night,
A silent waltz, pure and white.
Bare branches reach for the starry sky,
In winter's grasp, the world stands by.

Quiet whispers fill the frozen air,
Nature sleeps beneath its blanket rare.
Footprints trace a path so fine,
In the unseen dance, all seems divine.

Frosty breath, exhaled with pride,
Echoes of warmth where dreams reside.
Each flake a story, unique and grand,
In winter's arms, we understand.

The chill wraps round like a soft sigh,
Embracing moments that swiftly fly.
Under the stars, we're drawn to glance,
In the stillness, we find our chance.

Nature's ballet, a precious find,
In winter's heart, we're intertwined.
Through silent nights, we find our way,
In this unseen dance, we choose to stay.

Glimmering Pathways in the Chill

Under the frost, the ground does gleam,
A glimmering path, like a dream.
Each step lights up with a spark,
Guiding spirits through the dark.

Moonbeams dance on the icy streams,
Reflecting hopes and whispered dreams.
Branches bow to the winter's grace,
In this beauty, we find our place.

Crystals sparkle, a fairy's flight,
Painting the world in pure delight.
Nature's canvas, adorned with care,
Glimmering whispers fill the air.

Footsteps echo in the quiet night,
A journey taken, hearts unite.
Through the chill, we hold on tight,
To glimmering pathways, oh so bright.

In every corner, warmth is found,
Softly wrapped in magic's sound.
Together we roam, side by side,
On glimmering pathways, where dreams abide.

Mysteries of the Midwinter Night

Beneath the cloak of a midnight sky,
Where shadows whisper and secrets lie.
Stars emerge like jewels hidden away,
In the mysteries of night, dreams sway.

A soft hush falls on the sleeping earth,
Inviting wonders of timeless birth.
The moon shines bright, a guiding light,
Unveiling magic in the heart of night.

Crisp air dances with secrets untold,
Embracing dreams both shy and bold.
Each breath we take, a sacred rite,
In the mysteries of midwinter's night.

Softly the world begins to breathe,
In every corner, tales we weave.
With open hearts, we tread so right,
Exploring the wonders that shine so bright.

Wrapped in stillness, we find our voice,
In winter's realm, we can rejoice.
For in the mysteries, we ignite,
A fire within on this tranquil night.

Dance of the Winter's Breath

Snowflakes twirl in silent grace,
Whispered secrets, soft embrace,
Frosty air, a chilling song,
Nature's dance, the night is long.

Branches draped in silver gleam,
Frozen rivers, softly beam,
Moonlit paths, a tranquil sight,
Guiding dreams through winter's night.

Crisp the crunch beneath our feet,
Hearts aglow with warmth, we meet,
In the hush, a magic shared,
Life's pure beauty, unprepared.

Candles flicker, shadows play,
Cozy corners, soft ballet,
Winter whispers, tales untold,
In its grasp, our spirits hold.

Together in this frosty air,
A chance to pause, to breathe, to care,
In the dance of winter's breath,
Find the warmth that conquers death.

When the Twilight Shimmers

Stars begin to twinkle bright,
Casting dreams in fading light,
Whispers of the day now part,
Twilight colors every heart.

Shadows stretch on evening's glow,
Soft winds rise and gently blow,
Dancing leaves, a lullaby,
Time to pause and simply sigh.

Crimson skies, a fleeting show,
As the sun begins to slow,
In the hush of dusk we stand,
Life's embrace, a gentle hand.

Night will cloak our cares away,
Dreams will weave through night and day,
In the shimmer, hope resides,
Carried by the evening tides.

Together, hearts in sync will beat,
Underneath the stars, so sweet,
When the twilight starts to glow,
Love's true colors start to show.

The Hush of Icy Eves

Whispers wrapped in frosty night,
Stars above, a stunning sight,
Silent woods in heavy shrouds,
Nature bows beneath the clouds.

Footsteps soft on snowflakes white,
Echoes fade with each delight,
Breezes carry scents of pine,
In this hush, the world aligns.

Glistening branches bow and sway,
In the stillness, night holds sway,
Crystals spark on windowpanes,
Winter speaks in quiet strains.

Dreams of warmth beneath our skin,
Fires crackle, stories spin,
Gathered close, we share our fears,
In the hush, love perseveres.

Underneath the stars' embrace,
Finding peace, a sacred space,
In the hush of icy eves,
Hope and joy are what we weave.

Below the Glistening Overhead

Moonlight dances on the lake,
Silver ripples softly wake,
Stars reflect on waters deep,
Nature sings, our hearts to keep.

In the quiet, shadows blend,
Time stands still, as night does mend,
Beneath the sky's vast, shimm'ring veil,
Every breath, a soothing tale.

Cool winds whisper through the trees,
Carrying a soft, sweet breeze,
Carpet of leaves, a gentle rustle,
In this beauty, hearts will bustle.

Underneath the heavens wide,
With each moment, souls collide,
Magic swirls in quiet tones,
Lonely whispers turn to moans.

Below the glistening overhead,
Dreams are cast, and fears are shed,
In the glow of starlit night,
We find our paths, our hearts take flight.

9 789916 796481